Children
on the Loose

Collected by

murray watts

MONARCH
BOOKS

Mill Hill, London NW7 3SA and Grand Rapids, Michigan 49501

First published by Monarch Books in the UK 1999. This edition 2001.
Concorde House, Grenville Place, Mill Hill, London NW7 3SA.
Published in the USA by Monarch Books 2001.

Distributed by:
UK: STL, PO Box 300, Kingstown Broadway, Carlisle, Cumbria CA3 0QS;
USA: Kregel Publications, PO Box 2607 Grand Rapids, Michigan 49501.

ISBN 1 85424 511 2 (UK)
ISBN 0 8254 5996 6 (USA)

British Library Cataloguing Data
A catalogue record for this book is available from the British Library.

Cartoons by Darren Harvey Regan

Designed and produced for the publishers by
Gazelle Creative Productions,
Concorde House, Grenville Place, Mill Hill, London NW7 3SA.
Printed in Singapore.

The headmaster made an impromptu visit to a junior classroom. The pupils sweated with fear as he fired questions, one after another, which they failed to answer.

'Who made the world?' the headmaster raised his voice threateningly.

'Children,' he bent over the front row,

'I want to know who made the world.'

A small boy blurted out in terror,

'Oh sir, please sir, it wasn't me.'

A minister, arriving as a visiting speaker to a neighbouring church, decided to take a very informal approach with the children. Word had reached him of the strict and pious atmosphere of the Sunday school, and he decided he would introduce a refreshing change of approach.

Sitting on the edge of a desk, wearing an open-necked shirt, he leaned confidentially towards the children. 'Can anyone tell me,' he asked them, 'what is small, grey, eats nuts and has a large bushy tail?'

There was a long silence, then one small boy put up his hand and said, 'I know the answer should be Jesus, but it sounds like a squirrel to me.'

During a long and very boring sermon, a small but distinct voice could be heard at the back of the church, asking: 'Mummy, is it *still* Sunday?'

On another occasion, I was at a church service with members of my family. My aunt had been away for a while and she had two envelopes for the collection plate. She gave one to her four-year-old grandson. When the plate came to her, he whispered, 'It's all right, Gran, I've paid for you.'

A family was entertaining some pious friends for dinner.

The hostess, keen to show that they upheld Christian standards in their own home, asked her five-year-old son to say grace.

He looked blank.

There was an awkward pause, followed by a reassuring smile from the boy's mother.

'Well, darling, just say what Daddy said at breakfast this morning.'

Obediently, the boy repeated, 'Oh God, we've got those awful people coming for dinner tonight.'

The junior form was doing a project on the Creation.

George, aged seven, wrote:

'God made the first man and called him *Adam*. Then God made the first woman and called her *Madam*.'

During a family communion service at a church in York two little boys went up to the altar rail with their parents. As the minister passed along the line, giving bread to the adults and blessing the children, one little boy looked hungrily at the loaf.

His brother whispered, *'Go on, give him a bit, it's his birthday!'*

'God doesn't love me,' cried the little girl.
'Don't be silly,' said her father, 'of course
he does!'
She refused to be comforted.
'I know he doesn't because I tried him
with a daisy.'

Little girl:	**Does God make lions, Mummy?**
Mother:	**Yes, dear.**
Little Girl:	**But isn't he *frightened* to?**

13

A LITTLE GIRL SCREAMED and came running into her mother. 'There's a tiger in the garden!'

The mother jumped up and tore back the curtains.

A St Bernard was wandering slowly across the lawn.

'That's not a tiger,' she said, 'that's Billy Smith's dog from over the road. You know perfectly well it isn't a tiger. Go and ask God to forgive you for telling such a lie!'

Obediently, the little girl went upstairs. A few minutes later she came down smiling.

'Well,' said her mother, 'did you ask God to forgive you for telling a lie?'

'Yes,' she replied, 'and God said it was okay.'

'Okay?'

'Yes, God said the first time he saw Billy Smith's dog, he thought it was a tiger, too!'

A mother was entertaining guests when her five-year-old son began talking to a fly.

'Do you know that God loves you, little fly?' he asked, gently.

Everyone was deeply touched by this.

'And do you love God, little fly?' said the budding St Francis.

The boy's mother had tears in her eyes.

'Would you like to go to God, little fly?' the boy persisted.

The guests looked at him in admiration.

'Then go to God, little fly!' said the boy and squashed it.

A little girl was on her first visit to church,
where she saw the congregation kneeling
down to pray.
'What are they doing, Mummy?' she asked,
'They're praying, dear.'
'Praying?'
She began to giggle.
'What, with all their clothes on!?'

A woman, walking her dog on Clifton Downs in Bristol, met my god-daughter, aged three.

She looked at Joanna, who was wearing a pair of blue dungarees, and said to her mother, 'What a lovely little boy.'

Joanna turned straight to the woman's dog and said loudly,

'Hello, pussy.'

Baptism has lost some of its significance in societies where it is fashionable to 'have the baby done'.

The most extreme example of meaningless ritual was the case of a woman who arrived on the doorstep of the local minister in Liverpool, handed him her baby and said, 'Please could you christen him while I do the shopping?'

The following lines are quoted from a children's nativity play when Mary and Joseph approach the innkeeper who tells them there is no room in the inn.

Joseph: But my wife is pregnant
Innkeeper: Well, it's not my fault
Joseph: It's not my fault either!

Schoolroom howlers

A gargoyle is seen on church towers
and people's necks.
They come,
whether you like it or not.

Jesus appeared to two disciples behind locked doors as they were walking to Emmaus.

*A lie is a sin
and an abomination
in the sight of the Lord,
but a very present help
in time of trouble.*

**John the Baptist
was beheaded with
the Axe of the Apostles.**

**You must love your neighbour
even if you hate him.**

Question: What is a vixen?
Answer: A lady vicar.

*Everyone was pleased
when Jesus healed
the paralytic man,
except Simon
who had to pay
to have the roof mended.*

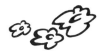

'Three shots rang out.
Two of the servants fell dead
and the other
went through his hat.'

'Christians are only allowed one wife
and this is known as monotony.'

Question: Write down what you know about Elijah.

Answer: All I know about Elijah is that he went for a cruise with a widow.

Question: Write what you know about the Last Supper.

Answer: I was away for that. I had measles.

Get the hens, Satan.

Four men came carrying
a parable on a bed.

Jesus said to the man at the pool,
'If you are good
and get a good job
and repent after you are healed,
God will heal you.'

If someone slaps you
turn and let him
have another knock
and the door shall be opened.

Two Jesuits,
probably a man and wife,
were on the way to Emmaus.

Jesus healed ten leopards and the one that lost his spots came back to thank him.

*It's hard for a man
with a camel in his eye
to walk into a needle
as for the man
to give up his wealth.*

Thy rod
and thy staff
they come for me.

Question: What is the first and greatest Commandment?

Answer: Hang all the law and the prophets.

Question: Who lived in the Garden of Eden?

Answer: The Adamses.

Lay not up for yourselves

trousers on earth.

A man came to the edge
of the volcano.
He looked over and saw
the creator smoking.

Jacob, son of Isaac, stole his brother's birthmark.

The end of the world
will mark a turning point
in everyone's life.

John said it was not awful
for you to marry
your brother's wife.

A MOTHER DECIDED TO start going to St Matthew's Church. She took her four-year-old son with her.

At first, the little boy was nervous of the church and especially of the minister, who had long hair, a beard and a booming voice. But he was a very good speaker and always entertained the children. Soon the little boy was looking forward eagerly to the Sunday morning services.

One Sunday he was utterly bewildered to find that the minister was away and instead there was a clean-shaven and rather dull guest speaker.

'Oh, Mummy,' he whispered, 'whatever's happened to St Matthew?'

With children there are problems
right from the word 'go'.
As the comedian said:

'I was born at home.
It was when my mother saw me
she was taken to hospital.'

And:

'When I was born,
the midwife took one look at me
and slapped my mother.'

A clergyman was taking tea with the farmer's wife when her children rushed in with a cardboard box.

'Mum!' They shouted triumphantly. 'We've trapped the rat!'

'Is it dead?' she asked anxiously.

'Oh, it's dead all right,' said the youngest boy. 'We beat it and beat it and beat it until-' Suddenly he noticed the clergyman's disapproving gaze.

'Until - er...' his voice dropped to a whisper, 'until the Lord called it home.'

THE VICAR AND HIS WIFE had left for a conference abroad, forgetting to give instructions for the banner which was to decorate the hall at the Christmas Carol Concert, the following weekend.

The secretary of the Mothers' Union was astonished to receive a telegram from France which read simply:

UNTO US A SON IS BORN.
NINE FEET LONG AND THREE FEET WIDE.
REV AND MRS JOHNSON.

A divinity teacher was explaining
the Creation story to his class.
One awkward little boy - always
a thorn in his side - called out:
'Please sir, my father says
we are descended from the apes.'
But this time the teacher
was ready for him.
'Carruthers,' he snapped,
'your family problems
are no concern of ours.'

A father was taking his thirteen-year-old
to task for smoking in the garden shed.
'And what about you,' he said,
turning to his ten-year-old daughter.
'Have you been smoking too?'
'No, Daddy,' she said,
with righteous indignation.
'I certainly have not.
I have given it up.'

A YOUNG COUPLE, WHO HAD many financial difficulties, found themselves facing another pregnancy. They already had three boys and so a fourth child was considered a disaster by the husband. However, his wife comforted him with the possibility of a little daughter - this pregnancy 'felt different.'

She decided to make this birth as special as possible and have the baby at home. Husband and midwife were in attendance and, sure enough, the pregnancy was different.

Very different. She had twins. Needless to say, they were both boys.

A little while later, the midwife went downstairs and met three-year-old George, up till then 'the baby of the family'. She explained to him that he now had two new little brothers.

'Oh,' said George nonchalantly, 'I know all about them.'

'Really?' said the nurse.

'Yes, and I know their names too.'

'Oh now, said the midwife smiling, 'you can't possibly know their names yet.'

'Oh, I do,' said George. 'I heard Daddy coming down the stairs saying "Hell and Damnation!"'

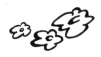

A young lad was becoming rather
restless during a church service.
His mother leaned down:
'Sssh,' she said,
'this is God's House.'
'Well,' said the boy,
'if I were God, I'd move.'

A sweet little girl of three knocked her
six-year-old brother out with a punch.
Her mother gasped in horror. 'Katie!
How *could* you do such a thing?'
'The Lord gave me strength,'
replied Katie proudly.

Teacher: **Now, Jenny, can you tell me the name of a well-known animal that supplies us with food and clothing?**

Jenny: **Yes. Daddy.**

According to psychiatrists, the first six months of our lives determine many things - in which case, my sister has something to worry about. When she was only a few weeks old, my father tripped on the top stair and lobbed her all the way down.

My uncle Hilbre, a GP, happened to be standing in the hall at the time. As my sister lay there, bawling her head off, he scarcely looked up. 'It's only when they don't cry you need to worry,' he said.

(Uncle Hilbre was always calm in the face of a crisis. It was he who said, 'Watch this for precision driving,' before wedging his car between two trams in the city centre of Liverpool.)

I suppose my father could have given the ultimate response to my sister's tumble:

'Come quickly, dear, our little girl's just taken her first twenty-five steps!'

There was a blinding flash of
lightning and Emily, aged five, rushed into
the house, shouting:
'Mummy, Mummy,
God has just taken my picture!'

Everyone can sympathise
with the desperate and doomed
prayer of the schoolboy
emerging from a geography exam:
'Dear God, please, *please*,
make Paris the capital of Turkey.'

A speaker at a Harvest Family Service
asked the children to name some of
the things they saw on display.
'Carrots,' said one.
'Potatoes,' said another.
'Peas,' said a third.
'Good,' said the speaker.
'Now can anyone give me a word
that covers all these things?'
'Gravy!' was the prompt reply.

A BISHOP WAS COMING TO STAY at a vicar's house for the night. The vicar had an eight-year old son, who was very excited about the important guest and begged his father to allow him to take the bishop his tea in the morning.

Eventually, the vicar agreed, but told his son that he must knock on the door and say, 'It's the boy, my Lord. It's time to get up.'

On the way upstairs the nervous boy was clutching the cup and saucer and practising the words his father had given him.

He knocked on the door and the bishop asked, 'Who is it?'

The boy replied at the top of his voice, 'It's the Lord, my boy. Your time is up!'

Teacher: **Who was most unhappy when the Prodigal Son came home?**

Pupil: **The fatted calf.**

65

A small boy, asked by his mother to pray for fine weather to make Granny's rheumatism better, came up with this memorable prayer:
'Oh Lord, please make it hot for Grandma!'

One woman to another:
'I want my children to have all
the things I couldn't afford -
then I shall move in with them.'

I can't help admiring one little boy who
summed up the problem of evil memorably.
His pious grandmother caught him
beating up his sister.
'Billy,' she said, leaning over him
and shaking her finger,
'it was Satan who told you to scratch
Catherine's face!'
'Perhaps it was,' said Billy,
'but it was my idea
to kick her in the shins.'

A little girl's father was going to sea. She prayed: 'Dear Lord, please watch over my Daddy. And,' she added, 'while you're at it, you'd better keep an eye on Mummy too.'

Soon after the Dead Sea Scrolls were discovered, a small boy was listening to the radio. He looked at his father anxiously.

'I hope they haven't found any more commandments.'

The following notice
in a church newsletter
could have been better expressed:
'Children are normally collected
during the Offertory Hymn.'

More howlers

A certain man drew his bow at a venture but missed the venture and hit Ahab.

An epistle is the wife of an apostle.

Whenever David played to Saul, the latter kept a javelin handy.

Joseph had a goat
of many colours,
but it got him out of the pit all right.

In the book of Job,
Satan is no ordinary devil.
He is the Attorney-General.

Q. Who said: 'What mean ye by these stones?'

A. It was said by Goliath to David.

He was dressed in
the garbage of a monk.

The chief missile of the Church of England is the Prayer Book.

Elijah was known as the Fishbite.
No one knows why.

The crusades were fought in plasticine.

You shall not admit adultery.

*A horse divided against itself
cannot stand.*

*You can tell a Gothic Cathedral
by its flying buttocks.*

Peter warmed his hands
at a damsel.

*Sins of omission are those
we have forgotten
to commit.*

*Mary Magdalene returned to
the womb but found it empty.*

*Thomas à Becket met Henry on
the altar steps and said:
'What ho, King!'
Henry massacred him
severely.*

*A deacon is a mass
of inflammable material
placed in a prominent
position to warn the people.*

Q. Who said: See that thou fall not out by the way'?

A. Elisha to Elijah when the latter went up to heaven in a chariot.

A casserole is a garment chiefly worn by curates.

*Solomon had 300 wives
and 700 porcupines.*

*Noah was the man who
danced before the ark,
but he first sent the bird away.*

*The Sadducees did not believe in
spirits, but the Publicans did.*

*Every year the Pope sent
missionaries to invert
the Chinese.*

*A pessimist is a man
who is never happy
unless he is miserable.
Even then he isn't happy.*

A sackbut is a large measure
of wine, much favoured
in biblical times.

When the dinner bell went
all the monks would crow
outside the refectory.

Eliza came before the king wrapped in a camel's hair and said: 'Behold me, I am Eliza the Tit-bit.'

An octopus is a person who hopes for the best.

B.C.   Before Christ
A.D.   After the Devil

After I had been in the Scouts a month,
I was publicly unrolled.

The prevailing religion in England
is hypocrisy.

Question: **What is an unclean spirit?**

Answer: **A dirty devil**

The Prodigal Son was a bit of a swine, but not near his father.